- Vol. 1 -

STARTING STRONG

Growing a
STRONG
Marriage

- *Vol. 1* -
STARTING STRONG

STUDY GUIDE BY AMY MCGOWAN

HENDRICKSON
PUBLISHERS

Growing a Strong Marriage (Vol. 1)—Starting Strong

© 2015 Hendrickson Publishers Marketing, LLC
P. O. Box 3473
Peabody, Massachusetts 01961-3473

ISBN 978-1-61970-584-5

Unless otherwise indicated, Scripture quotations are from The Holy Bible, English Standard Version® (ESV®), copyright © 2001 by Crossway, a publishing ministry of Good News Publishers. Used by permission. All rights reserved.

Printed in the United States of America

Second Printing — May 2015

Contents

Introduction to Growing a Strong Marriage

Welcome to Growing a Strong Marriage! Over the next few weeks we hope to strengthen and challenge you in your marriage as you go on this journey together with the other couples in your Bible study group.

This study on marriage is a unique one. You have been invited to hear stories from people who you probably already know and respect. Perhaps you have read their books, and now you have the opportunity to hear directly from them and their spouses on one of the most important aspects of their lives: marriage. Marriage has its difficulties and its joys. As two people journey through life together, they experience many different circumstances and learn more about each other and themselves. Whether you have been married for a few years or thirty years, there is always more to learn about each other and room to grow as a couple.

What is this series about? It is about creating an opportunity for you to grow a strong marriage so that when life's distractions and difficulties come your way, you will be rooted together in Christ and confident that you both are committed to making this marriage work. Through the videos, discussion with fellow couples in your group, and Bible study, we hope that truth will penetrate your marriage and provide nutrients that continue to enrich growth far beyond these next few weeks.

Know that this series is not a quick fix that will make all your marriage troubles go away. Rather it is a starting point for deeper communication and understanding with each other. No one ever said marriage would be easy, but it is certainly worth the effort. Also know that this series is not meant to be a solution to serious crises that sometime find their way into a marriage, such as adultery, violence, or addiction, to name a few. If you are facing any of these more serious issues, it is strongly encouraged that you seek good marriage counseling to help you work through them. If you need recommendations, your pastor can provide referral options. It is best if both attend counseling.

The Growing a Strong Marriage series is divided into three sections. The first study guide covers the biblical foundations of marriage. The second study guide addresses communication and conflict and has a bonus session on remarriage. The third and final study guide covers children, unexpected challenges, and staying connected, and has a bonus session on adoption. The sessions and study guides can be used individually or out of order, but it is recommended that they be completed in the order they are presented.

Over these next few weeks, we will learn from couples such John and Stasi Eldredge, Gary and Lisa Thomas, and Art and Lysa TerKeurst on how they handle conflict, communication, and life's difficulties. Chip and Theresa Ingram, Gordon and Gail MacDonald, and Les and Leslie Parrott will also join the conversation on topics such as the purpose of marriage, kids, and having fun together. Join them now in their living rooms, grab a cup of coffee, and listen to the stories and insights they have to share.

Introduction to Starting Strong

In this study guide and its videos, we will cover the biblical foundation of marriage. A house lasts long and stands strong when it is built on a solid foundation. You can work together to strengthen your relationship and how you view your marriage. This is where we will begin.

In the first session you will meet the six couples, get to know the other couples in your small group, and discuss the beginnings of marriage. The following session will focus on oneness and living in unity. Next, we will be reminded that although we are one, we are still individuals and children of God. In the final session of this study guide, we will look at the purpose of marriage as a way to make us more like Christ.

Let's begin!

How We Met

"It is not good that a man should be alone; I will make him a helper fit for him." (Genesis 2:18)

Each of the couples in the video is unique. They have their own personalities as individuals and as a couple. They have different ways of communicating and different senses of humor. But they also have something in common. These couples have been brought together on the video because at least one person in each couple has written multiple books. But what else do they have in common? All of these couples desire God to be first in their marriage. Some have had this goal from the beginning; others realized their deep need for the presence of God in their marriage a little later down the road. There should be a difference among Christians who are married. Each member must continuously grow and learn to better honor Christ and his or her spouse. As this study continues, you will see that each of these couples will show they are continually growing in this way.

Watch Session #1 now.

You have now met the six couples in the videos who are joining you in this study. Before we continue further, what is your story? Take a few moments to share with the group how you and your spouse first met. What were your first impressions of each other?

Marriage is a happy union filled with great joy and happiness, but that's not all. Marriage is also difficult and at times frustrating, as any couple married longer than six months can tell you.

Where did this idea of marriage begin? To find out, let's start at the very beginning.

Read Genesis 2:18–25.

Originally, Moses wrote the book of Genesis for the people of Israel. It is God's story that reminded the people of their identity in him. Imagine what it would have been like for them to tell this story to their children and how this would have sounded in their time. All the other peoples and nations around them had their own ideas and stories of how the earth came to be, which commonly began with gods fighting one another. In these stories, humanity was made as an afterthought or by accident and was intended to be the slaves of the gods, created to do their bidding and offer food and sacrifices to them. It was all about the unpredictable gods, what they wanted, and how to keep them appeased.

But the God of Israel is different. He is the one true God— Yahweh. He created the earth, but not just any earth. God created the earth to be ideal for human life. The creation of humanity is the climax of the Creation story, not an after-thought. We are made in the image of God. No other part of creation is made with this likeness. As Gordon Wenham says in *A Guide to the Pentateuch,* rather than people being created to bring God food, God makes food for the people. There are no other gods greater than he; Yahweh himself created all that exists. All of creation is good and when God created people, he declared it was "*very* good."

After all of creation is pronounced "good," something comes up as "not good": man is alone. What a harsh in-terruption to this beautiful creation story! The rivers are flowing, the grass is green, the fruit is ripe on the tree, but Adam is alone. God notices this and has a solution. God makes Adam a helper (2:18). But we should note that Eve is his helper, not his servant. Rather, *helper* is the same word also used to describe God himself when David sings, "You are my help and my deliverer" (Psalm 70:5; see also Psalms 33:20 and 115:9). This is no demeaning term, but one that shows how well man and woman fit together. No other part of creation could complement Adam. Eve is Adam's helper and companion. God introduced them to each other and they are joined in perfect unity.

In what way is your spouse your helper as we have talked about here?

If God then created marriage, what does a biblical marriage look like? This is a question all of these couples on the video have asked themselves and want you to ask the same. We will look at many different aspects of how a marriage grows strong, but let's first begin with the biblical foundation of marriage.

Marriage Is God's Idea

Marriage is not something that was socially constructed over time to be adjusted as culture's whims desired. Marriage is a beautiful gift from God designed by God. He is the one who can best show us what marriage was intended to be and what it means to be a good husband and wife.

In what ways do you think a Christian marriage should be different than a non-Christian marriage?

After God created man and woman, he gave the woman to the man, who then said, "This is now bone of my bone and flesh of my flesh" (Genesis 2:23). Although Adam had seen many other creatures and named each one, not one of them was a suitable helper or partner for him. Then one day Adam falls asleep. When he awakes, there's someone new standing right in front of him—someone who looks so much like him, yet still strikingly different . . . in a good way! She talks like him, walks like him, has skin and hair like him. In fact, they are made of the same stuff. She is bone of his bone, flesh of his flesh. God presents this woman to this man, and we have the beginning of marriage: "For this reason a man shall leave his father and his mother, and be joined to his wife, and they shall become one flesh."

Marriage Is for Companionship

God created Eve as an answer to Adam's loneliness. Adam was waiting for a companion who was like him and when God presented Eve to him, he said, "This is now bone of my bones and flesh of my flesh" (Genesis 2:23). She is so much like him that they are of the very same shared substance. He continues, "She shall be called Woman, because she was taken out of Man." In the original language, we can see how closely Adam associated Eve with himself: Man is *eesh* and Woman is *eesha*. Adam had already given names to all the animals and every living thing of creation. He now gives Woman her name and uses his own name to name her—this is how much he recognizes she is a part of him and what he has been waiting for. They were naked and not ashamed (2:25). There was no bitterness, no shame, no self-consciousness. They were fully exposed to each other, and all was perfect and right in the world. We do not know how long they had together like this before sin entered the world, but what a beautiful time it must have been.

*"It was only after . . . Stasi coming back to faith
in Christ [and] me coming to Christ that our
romance blossomed." —John Eldredge*

Marriage Is for Procreation

In Genesis 1:28, God commands Adam and Eve to "be fruitful and multiply, fill the earth, and subdue it." They are invited to play a critical role in creating and continuing life on earth, which can only happen through a man and woman as God designed it. Marriage is the starting point for creating a family that raises and nurtures children in the way of the Lord (Proverbs 22:6; Ephesians 6:4). Although one result of marriage is often raising children, we do live in a fallen world affected by sin and not all couples are able to conceive and give birth to children. But by the grace of God, husband and wife can have a happy and fulfilled marriage with or without children. Every healthy marriage has the potential to be a cornerstone of a healthy society and can positively affect generations to come.

A biblical understanding of marriage is that it was founded by God, made for companionship, and intended as the context for procreation. What are other aspects of a biblical marriage?

Take a short moment to share what your main take-away from this session has been.

Questions for Home

In each session there will be questions to discuss with the group as a whole. It is good to hear from each other to share experience and insight. But just as important is for you to talk privately as husband and wife about what the Lord may be teaching you. After all, the primary purpose of this study is for you to grow a stronger marriage. So each week, take time to discuss what stood out to you from that session. Maybe it's something you had never thought of before. Maybe there's something you want to talk about or build into your marriage. Use these questions to spark the conversation. Set aside a date night, some alone time, or even take the long way home and talk.

What are you hoping to get out of going through this study together?

Moving into Oneness

> Therefore a man shall leave his father and
> mother and hold fast to his wife and they
> shall become one flesh. (Genesis 2:24)

Remember back to your wedding day. Was it a big affair with all of your family and friends? Or was it a small, intimate ceremony with only the closest people? The wedding day is a happy one, full of joy, hope, and dreams. From that day onward, your life changed. You made a permanent, lifelong commitment to this person that no matter what, you would stick to the other's side—not because you *felt* like it, but because you *chose* to. That's love: more than feelings, it is a conscious choice.

Typically in Christian ceremonies, the minister talks about the couple as "the two becoming one," which comes from Genesis 2:24, or "what God has joined together, let no man separate" from Matthew 19:15. From that day forward the couple joins together into what Paul calls "that great mystery" (Ephesians 5:31–32) of marriage: that you are no longer two, but one.

When we left our fathers and mothers to be married, there were many uncertainties as we began our lives together. The single life is behind and joined life is ahead. What is one way that "becoming one" became more real to you after you were married?

Watch Session #2 now.

In a culture in which the importance of marriage is on the decline, is defined more and more loosely, and can be seen as temporary, it can be easy to lose sight of its beginnings, original purpose, and significance. Marriage is both a covenant and a commitment. It's not a contract that has a certain term or can be terminated when circumstances are no longer ideal, but it is a covenant very much like the covenants made by God with his people. It's a vow to love your spouse even when he or she is not loveable. After all, God made his covenant with Abraham not because he deserved it, but because God chose to. Jesus died for sinners not because we are so good and loveable, but because he loved us and chose to.

Marriage is not easy and that's because it consists of two selfish sinners intimately sharing life together. Who could expect that to go perfectly? There's nothing "easy" about it. But this is what gives the covenant and vows their incredible meaning and depth. You're telling your spouse, "No matter what—if you're sick and can't even take care of yourself, or we're so poor we don't know what we're going to eat tomorrow, or we just can't seem to see eye to eye on life right now—I am going to stick with you and we're going to get through this together. I'm not going anywhere. And I know and trust you have made the same vow to me. When life gets the absolute hardest, you're still going to be here. When all else of life is falling apart, we won't. Even when the stress gets so overwhelming that we turn on each other rather than turn together against the problem, we will step back and remember our covenant. Even when I really am at fault and cause pain, there is grace and forgiveness and our covenant relationship will endure." That's when vows matter the most—in the hard times. Vows aren't tested when life is easy.

May this not become cliché or too familiar. Reflect on how powerful this is! Imagine if instead these were your vows on that happy day: "I take you to be my husband/wife. I promise to love you and to cherish you as long as I'm happy and feel this is working out. I promise to be with you forever—as long as I feel you are giving me what I deserve. I vow to be your companion in life as long as I feel that I still love you. If any of this changes, I consider this marriage null and void." Those aren't vows and are hardly worth saying. There's no meaning there. Yet how often do these "vows" reflect the popular understanding of true marriage commitment under the surface?

In light of these non-vows, what is the significance of the real vows spoken at most wedding ceremonies? What difference does it make knowing your spouse has promised to be with you no matter what?

Permanent vows and lasting covenants are not easy to keep. Many unexpected challenges arise. People change over time and the feelings of love are fluid. How can someone possibly have strength to get through such difficult and straining times? There is one truth important to remember: there is a third person in this covenant. A Christian marriage is not just husband and wife, but husband and wife and God. He has bound you together and the presence of his Holy Spirit fills you with his love, patience, kindness, goodness, faithfulness, gentleness, and self-control (Galatians 5:22–23). The presence of God within marriage is what makes a Christian marriage so unique.

When man and wife become one, they no longer live separate lives. They no longer depend on the families they grew up in for economic or social support. They have joined together and become one as God intended. In Matthew 19, the Pharisees question Jesus whether a man can divorce his wife for any reason. Jesus responds,

> *"Have you not read that He who created them from the beginning made them male and female, and said 'For this reason a man shall leave his father and mother and be joined to his wife, and the two shall become one flesh'? So they are no longer two, but one flesh. What therefore God has joined together, let no man separate."*
>
> *(Matthew 19:4–6)*

He emphasizes that the original intention and plan of marriage is inseparable unity. Although divorce was permissible in cases of adultery, it wasn't the norm and certainly not the plan. The Pharisees wanted to focus on rules governing divorce and missed God's intention for marriage, but Jesus focused on marriage, unity, and oneness. This is God's intention for marriage.

This oneness is manifested ultimately in the physical union that consummates the marriage. In what other ways have you become one in your marriage?

In the video the couples talk about various reasons for getting married. Why did you get married? Why didn't you stay single? (Don't feel you have to give the perfect answer; be honest.)

"You've got to have a vision beyond your mailbox." —Art TerKeurst

There are many important reasons to get married. You may have shared that you love each other, you are best friends, you want to share life together, you want to raise a family together, or you have fun and laugh together. These are all good and important aspects that should be present. But the MacDonalds and TerKeursts encourage you to take it a step further: marriage has to be about more than babies and white picket fences. It is important to have a shared unified vision for life.

Ask yourself: Do you both desire the same things? Are you working toward the same goal? Do you share the same core vision and purpose for life? Is it important for you to have an impact outside of yourselves as a couple? If so, in what way?

What are some examples of a core vision that a married couple might share?

Having a shared vision is not only a future idea but is very much a present reality as well. Depending on where you are in life, you may define your shared vision as something to do in the future or an impact you want to make someday. Maybe you find yourselves thinking, "Once we have a house, or once we have a child, or once the kids are gone, or once we make a certain amount of money—*then* we can really serve God together, really have time to grow closer, and do things that will make our marriage better for ourselves and for other people." But let this be a challenge to share a common vision *now*.

What does the Lord have for you as a couple today? What are you able to do better together that you would not have been able to do alone?

Let's take this a step further. There is a difference between being one in marriage and actually living in that oneness. Oneness doesn't happen on its own, but is something you have to fight for and maintain. Lysa and Art TerKeurst have a great way of thinking about this. They talk about a "continuum" and refer to "oneness" as this unified way of being and living together.

"Isolation" is living so emotionally and mentally separate from each other that little to nothing is shared. A couple in isolation will likely feel completely alone and unsupported. "Drifting" falls somewhere in between. You likely don't hold anything against each other, but in the mundane rhythms and business of life, you are "like two ships passing in the night." Naturally, for most couples, this drifting stage is the easiest stage to fall into by default..

Isolation	Drifting	Oneness

What are some words you would use to describe each of these states?

Isolation:

Drifting:

Oneness:

Most couples go through many of the same life stages: dating, engagement, newlyweds, babies, new careers, teenagers, challenges, empty nest, retirement, and so many other unique stages in between. Life changes can have a significant impact on your marriage, but happily you have each other to navigate these changes together. The TerKeursts' way of evaluating their relationship on this continuum is helpful for describing where you are and how close you are. Where are we? Where do we want to be? What will we do to get there? It is important to talk about this together. The first step toward oneness is acknowledging you're not there but that you want to be. If one of you doesn't feel like you're living in oneness, but the other thinks everything is fine, you probably are not. If you are, both of you will know.

Life makes it fairly easy to move to the left toward drifting and isolation, doesn't it? What sorts of things can move you that direction and pull you away from each other?

Moving to the right toward oneness takes more intentionality and determination. It's easy to get pulled downstream as life just happens: busy schedules, kids, responsibilities, church activities, work. But it takes effort to set aside the distractions and make time to invest in each other. What can help you move toward oneness together?

In the video, the Ingrams modeled something that is crucial in maintaining oneness: gratefulness. One of the quickest ways to drift apart is to be critical of each other. We all do things that drive each other crazy. Early in the relationship that "one thing" may have been "cute," but now it's like fingernails on a chalkboard. Maybe her organization is great, but sometimes it just feels so restricting. Maybe he's great at having fun at the spur of the moment and you loved that when you were dating, but now it seems he can't plan anything. Chip Ingram used to feel this way. But then he realized she's a "package deal" and he shouldn't be critical of a part of the package—he needs to love it all. Without some of the parts, Theresa wouldn't be Theresa.

Do nothing from selfishness or empty conceit, but with humility of mind regard one another as more important than yourselves; do not merely look out for your own interests, but also for the interests of others. (Philippians 2:3–4)

Celebrate the differences and laugh at them together. Understanding each other's personalities and sense of humor is vital to any marriage. You have a choice as to how you choose to respond to these quirks: Do you see them as silly and endearing, or horribly annoying? Differences create uniqueness. Besides, do you *really* want your spouse to be *exactly* like you?

There is great freedom in the relationship when you accept your spouse just as he or she is—and when you know your spouse accepts you for exactly who you are. Now, we are by no means perfect, and personal growth does happen and needs to happen in marriage. But for those little idiosyncrasies, let's not be critical but instead choose to be thankful. For those things that do need to be transformed, let's give each other grace, just as God gives grace to us.

What we choose to focus on can greatly affect the picture we hold of our spouse and how we respond to each other. This doesn't mean you should be blind or unrealistic, but do look at the whole person. Choose not to be critical of the few things when you can be so thankful for the many.

Finally, brothers, whatever is true, whatever is honorable, whatever is just, whatever is pure, whatever is lovely, whatever is commendable, if there is any excellence, if there is anything worthy of praise, think about these things. (Philippians 4:8)

Your spouse is an amazing person. What is one thing you greatly love and respect about your spouse? Briefly share this with the group.

One of the most unifying and healthy things you can do in your marriage is to pray together. Some families pray over meals and this is a good habit, but it is also good and beneficial for couples to pray together on their own. Some may already do this and that's great. But if you do not, let this be a challenge to do so during the weeks of this study. You can decide whether this means daily, weekly, or a couple times a week. Decide the time best for both of you when you will not be distracted, and then put it in your schedule.

If you haven't prayed together much, you may feel uncomfortable at first. If so, how can you pray together and not feel awkward? Just pray together anyway and do it again the next day. Experience will make it more natural. If you need a place to start, share with each other something you're thankful for and something you're concerned about. Then pray for each other and for your marriage. It doesn't have to be long and you don't have to use special words. It's not a magic formula or a tool, but through it you are able to set aside your busy schedule, spend valuable quality time with your spouse, and intentionally invite God to be present in your marriage—reminding yourselves that he is your Father and the One who has given you to each other.

Other prayer points for over the next few weeks:

- Thank God for your spouse.

- Pray that God will grow and strengthen your marriage.

- Pray about those areas that hinder oneness in your marriage. Ask God for the resolve to engage in what will foster oneness.

- Pray that God will humble you and show you how to be a better wife or husband.

- Pray that outside forces will not attack your marriage.

Look for ways to build each other up and to encourage each other. Some people are natural encouragers while others have to try a little harder, but it is still important to affirm your spouse in the way that he or she will feel most loved and appreciated. Spend time together. Do an activity together. Go for a walk. Be a safe place to share about your day, your thoughts, and your concerns. As you do, you will learn more about each other and grow closer together, as well as allow for an increase in physical, emotional, and spiritual intimacy. In the words of Lysa TerKeurst's Papaw: "If you find life, find it with God at the center and find it together."

Take a short moment to share what your main take-away from this session has been.

Questions for Home

What did you want in marriage when you were dating or first married? How has that developed or changed? Is there anything you want to bring back as a priority?

What is your shared vision now?

What things can you stand together against that might threaten oneness in your marriage?

Describe times in your marriage when you were in isolation, drifting, oneness. What stage are you in right now? If you both don't feel you're in oneness, what's one thing you can do this week that will help move you in that direction? If you already feel you're in oneness, what's one thing you can do this week to protect and deepen that?

Identity in Christ

But to all who did receive him, who believed
in his name, he gave the right to become
children of God, who were born, not of
blood nor of the will of the flesh nor of the
will of man, but of God. (John 1:12–13)

Watch Session #3 now.

Can you resonate with the Eldredges's story? They were
in love and saw each other as a real gift from God. They
were happy and thankful for each other. Stasi gave John a
journal in their early years and in it he wrote that she is his
"true gift."

Yet there was something still not quite right. She was often
disappointed when he fell short of her expectations, and he
was discouraged that he let her down. This led to further
frustration and tension, only to be repeated again down
the road.

This happens in many marriages and it's no surprise. As
John Eldredge points out, culture tells us through movies, books, and television that marriage is supposed to be
"amazing." Not to mention, many churches paint a picture
of marriage as perfect and, indeed, amazing. And marriage
certainly can be wonderful. In fact, this study is all about

growing a strong and great marriage together. There's nothing wrong with that! But John Eldredge is specifically referring to the needless pressure for marriage to be "amazing" all the time. What is this "amazing"? Always blissfully happy, never fighting, always agreeing, immediately seeing each other's point of view, thinking of each other first. Nothing goes wrong—ever. Again, all good things, but realistic? No.

Your spouse is still human and is not going to live up to unrealistic expectations. While this is probably no surprise to you, it is worth remembering. It's so easy to get frustrated with each other, especially if it's related to a repeated occurrence. But what difference can it make to keep in mind that your spouse is not perfect and neither are you?

"My biggest unrealistic expectation was expecting Art to know how to fix me." —Lysa TerKeurst

Let's take a step back for a moment. Whether verbalized or not, there's often an expectation that marriage is supposed to be bliss. When it isn't, frustration grows. But why get frustrated? Because expectations are not being met. So let's take a look first at expectations.

Before getting married, everyone has his or her own idea of what life and marriage are going to look like. Many different factors help to paint this picture: parents, movies, television shows, society, and even the church. Probably the most significant influence, however, comes from within the family you grew up in. Some expectations are good and healthy. Some are unrealistic. Many times we don't even know what those expectations are until something happens that goes against an expectation and we react negatively.

Most expectations come to light within the first months and years of marriage, but other times they reveal themselves far later. Some are smaller issues that can be frustrating and might include cooking: is it one person's responsibility or something both do together? What about the toilet seat? Is he expected to put it down or leave it up? Should the bed be made daily or left alone? No doubt this will generate some response within the group!

These types of expectations—and others that are far more serious—can be worked out over time with some good communication and understanding. Others might not be so simple. The most challenging ones are those that are difficult to even put into words because they go unrecognized. The Eldredges talked about one unrealistic expectation that can be damaging to a marriage: expecting your spouse to be God.

"Even a great husband makes a very poor god."
—Lysa TerKeurst

But he or she is not God and never will be. This is a good thing. Your spouse would make a lousy god, so let him or her love you, faults and all; receive that love and show it back, knowing he or she has faults too. Only the one true God can love us perfectly and completely. When you identify each other as God's workmanship and not as God, you will find that your patience and grace toward each other will increase drastically.

For we are his workmanship, created in Christ Jesus for good works, which God prepared beforehand, that we should walk in them. (Ephesians 2:10)

When we put our spouse in place of God, we begin to unrealistically expect from our spouse that which only God can provide. These unrealistic expectations can manifest themselves in many ways. Perhaps these unrealistic expectations of your spouse might sound familiar:

- He/she will always complete me.
- He/she will always make me happy.
- He/she will always know how to make me feel better.
- He/she will always know what's wrong and how to fix it.
- He/she will always know what I need.
- He/she will always take care of me.
- He/she will always protect me and provide for me.
- He/she will never let me down.

Is there anything else that you can add to the list?

And it is God who establishes us with you in Christ, and has anointed us, and who has also put his seal on us and given us his Spirit in our hearts as a guarantee. (1 Corinthians 1:21–22)

You may not say these out loud, but some form of them may come to the surface from time to time without you even realizing it. Next time you get frustrated with your spouse, there certainly may be a real reason for you to feel that way and, if so, then you can work through it together. But also ask yourself first if this is stemming from an unrealistic expectation. If it is, maybe there's really no need to be frustrated, or at least not feel it as strongly as you do.

Stasi Eldredge came to this realization: John is not her god. She had him on such a high pedestal that she expected him to be perfect, just like Jesus. Then when he let her down or he was frustrated with her, her world fell apart. It was only after she came to understand her identity and acceptance in God, rather than in her husband, that these expectations were exposed and their marriage began to relax.

Who Am I?

Remember this: You were first a child of God before you were a husband or wife, and you will remain his child long after this life on earth. Even if you didn't trust in Christ until after you were married, you were first made in the image of God, and your ultimate identity has always first been in him as your Creator. To put anyone or anything before him is idolatry.

See what kind of love the Father has given to us, that we should be called children of God; and so we are. The reason why the world does not know us is that it did not know him. (1 John 3:1)

Not only were you created by God, in his image, but you were also redeemed by the blood of his Son! He has put a seal on you—you are guaranteed his forever. The Father's great love has adopted you as children of God. That's who you are. Husband and wife are first son and daughter of the Most High. You have already been fully accepted by him. He loves you, and you do not have to work for that love. It is already freely yours.

Stasi looked for acceptance in John, but it was when she learned that she is God's beloved that everything changed. Her self-worth and identity no longer were based on what her husband said or did. She could receive that ultimate core love that her soul most deeply longed for only from her Creator. Even when John and Stasi let each other down or did not feel completely accepted, they were now able to rest in their acceptance from God. Previously when they found their foundation and identity in each other, they had nothing to stand on when everything was shaky and falling apart. But now they can stand firm in him and work out their issues from this common foundation.

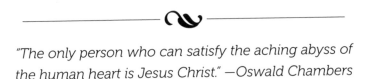

"The only person who can satisfy the aching abyss of the human heart is Jesus Christ." —Oswald Chambers

We can falsely find our identity in other things as well. Chip and Theresa Ingram shared an example of this from their lives. Chip had been directly involved with many ministries in his past. They had always done well, and many times he had been the one who turned a dying ministry into a thriving one. This was important to him and all good work. But then something happened. A ministry he had been working on for years just wasn't getting off the ground like he expected it would. He kept putting more time, more prayer, and more effort into it, but it just wasn't turning around. Failure was the elephant in the room, but he just couldn't accept it.

Through Theresa, Chip came to realize that he was putting this ministry first and that this was where he was trying to find his identity. Without it, he felt he would have to admit he was a failure and worthless. Yet Theresa reminded him that he was not a failure. He didn't have to work for his acceptance; God had already accepted him completely. He didn't have to work for love and respect; his family already loved and respected him. Putting this ministry to rest would not change any of that.

In the context of marriage, the idolatry of putting your spouse in the place of God is dangerous and can be an easy trap to fall into. Yet there are other areas in our lives that we yield to instead of God, which can directly impact our marriages. For example, in the case of Chip attempting to find his identity and acceptance in his ministry, it also put a strain on his marriage and family.

"God has taught me about his love through Theresa—that he accepts me completely and totally apart from my performance." —Chip Ingram

What are some other areas in which you may try to find your identity or acceptance rather than in God?

Spouse, ministry, work, and kids may be some of the most common responses. Most of what is important in our lives are not bad things. In fact, they are good things that have been given as gifts, skills, or even callings. The problem comes when they become too predominant in our lives and when we begin to find our identity in the gifts rather than the Giver.

Who Is My Spouse?

We've discussed that your identity is ultimately and completely in Christ, not in each other or your accomplishments. What else might this mean for your marriage? Just as you are God's beloved, so is your spouse. When husband and wife have their eyes first on Jesus and find their security and identity in him, they have great freedom! You're no longer expecting your spouse to be perfect, and you're not expected to be perfect. In John Eldredge's words, there is no longer a pressure to be "amazing." You each have the freedom to fail, to be human, to grow, to learn—together.

"God is my source of identity. This takes so much pressure off the marriage." —John and Stasi Eldredge

As you have seen, your spouse is a very poor god. He or she is never going to do everything right. Keeping this in mind will provide a different perspective when he or she lets you down next time. It's going to happen, so it doesn't have to come as such a surprise. But imagine what this can do for forgiveness and patience. Just as you've been given grace and been forgiven by God, so also you can extend grace and forgiveness to each other.

Finding your identity in Christ and your complete fulfillment in him enables you to now love and care for your spouse in a different way—with Christ's love. It's not your job to fix him or her. You can bring your spouse and his or her burdens or troubles to God in prayer, but only God has the power to change him or her.

Growing a Strong Marriage

What difference do you think it makes for your marriage when you find your identity in God rather than in your spouse?

Encourage each other in Christ as you desire to see each other walking with God. Remind each other of your identity in God, his love, acceptance, and grace, regularly saying, "You're not perfect and neither am I! But God is and he is the one who fills each of our hearts so that we can more fully love each other."

Two Are Better than One

"You complete me." You have probably heard this line often in the movies. It's sweet and nice to hear, but let's take a closer look at this statement. Does marriage complete you as if prior to marriage you were not a full person or something was missing of your core self? No, you were already complete because you were made in the image of God and as a Christian you have been redeemed and made whole.

Marriage is two complete people who continue to grow and are joined together by God. Two complete people are together with Christ as the head. God brings two unique individuals together. As each focuses on him, they can serve him together. God can do much with two people who are fixed on him with a common goal.

So how does this happen? As the Ingrams showed us, it's all about putting Jesus first. Time first with Jesus aligns not only your marriage, but all other priorities of life as well. You do not have to work for acceptance; you have already been accepted by God and are his child. Live in that identity as two individuals, complete in God, serving him together.

Take a short moment to share what your main take-away from this session has been.

Questions for Home

Have there been times in your marriage when you've realized you confused your spouse with Jesus?

It's easy to fall into trying to find our identity in something or someone other than God. Is there anything you can identify in your life that is a gift that has started to eclipse the Giver?

Paths to Christ in Marriage

Husbands, love your wives, as Christ loved
the church and gave himself up for her, that
he might sanctify her, having cleansed her
by the washing of water with the word, so
that he might present the church to himself
in splendor, without spot or wrinkle or any
such thing, that she might be holy and
without blemish. (Ephesians 5:25–27)

Holy matrimony. This is a fairly common phrase, often
used in the context of Christian weddings. What is it about
matrimony, or marriage, that is holy? Most poignant is
that marriage has been designed and instituted by God. He
introduced and initiated the first marriage with Adam and
Eve, and it has been highly regarded as holy throughout
church tradition ever since. A Christ-centered marriage
ought to look different from a secular marriage.

Watch Session #4 now.

Gordon MacDonald said that a shared vision for God is
what makes a marriage uniquely Christian. As Christians,
we desire for God to be glorified and for the world to know
him. God has given different people different desires and
passions to use in carrying out his mission in the world. But

what does a vision for God within a marriage specifically look like? Might marriage also be holy in that it develops holiness?

Read Ephesians 5:18–33.

There is much to learn about marriage in this passage, but first let's get a brief overview. The section on husbands and wives (Ephesians 5:26–33) is directly connected to the previous verses 18–21. Paul tells the Ephesians to be filled with the Spirit and to do the following (5:18–21):

- Sing psalms, hymns, and spiritual songs, and make music to the Lord;

- Give thanks for everything; and

- Submit to one another out of reverence for Christ.

To this last point Paul then connects the discussion of marriage. Husbands and wives are to submit to each other (5:21), with particular emphasis on reminding the wife to submit to her husband (vv. 22–24) and to respect him (v. 33). The husband is also reminded to love his wife (vv. 25, 28, 33).

"Marriage is designed to make you holy more than to make you happy."—Gary Thomas

Here Paul is not only talking about marriage, but he is also drawing a parallel with Christ and the church. The church submits to Christ just as the wife submits to the husband

(vv. 22–24), and the husband loves the wife just as Christ loves the church (vv. 25, 28–29). Neither submission nor loving as Christ loves is easy. Both require great self-sacrifice, selflessness, and love.

In what ways does the church submit to Christ? In what ways does Christ show love to the church?

Christ loved the church so much that he willingly gave himself up for her (Ephesians 5:25). This is the ultimate demonstration of love, submission, and humility. In the same way, husbands ought to love their wives with a humble and self-sacrificial love. It is within this nature of a relationship that we want to focus today.

What is the purpose of marriage? Marriage is about two people becoming one. At the center of a healthy marriage is a unified vision centered on God. A marriage is comprised of two individuals who find their core identity in God, rather than each other, and who continue to grow together. But what is the purpose? This same passage in Ephesians 5 speaks to this very question.

In Ephesians 5:25 we see that Christ loved the church and gave himself up for her. In Ephesians 5:26–27 there are three "purpose" statements that begin with "so that" or "that." Take a look at these statements that show the transformation that Christ's love brings:

- That he might sanctify her, having cleansed her by washing with the water of the word;

- That he might present the church to himself without spot or wrinkle; and

- That she might be holy and without blemish.

Christ gave himself for the church out of love, but that is only the tip of the iceberg. Loving the church includes desiring the best for her: that she would be holy, sanctified, and cleansed. She doesn't stay as she was, but becomes more like Christ. In the same way, the journey of every Christian is to become more like Christ. The marriage relationship is not only a picture of Christ and the church, but is also a place in which husband and wife are molded and shaped to be more like him.

"Therefore a man shall leave his father and mother and hold fast to his wife, and the two shall become one flesh." This mystery is profound and I am saying that it refers to Christ and the church. (Ephesians 5:31–32)

Marriage is a profound mystery. Two people come together in the closest and most intimate way, sharing all of life together. Furthermore, it mirrors Christ and the church. God is committed to our transformation to become holy and more like his Son, Jesus Christ. In Leviticus 11:44–45, God commands his people, "Be holy as I am holy." In 1 John 3:2–3 we are called children of God and are told to be pure as Christ is pure. And here in Ephesians we are again re-minded that Christ died for us so that we might be made holy. Being holy, becoming more like Christ, is obviously an important biblical theme.

If marriage is a reflection of Christ and the church, then in marriage we are transformed to become more like Christ. Just as Christ loved the church so that she may be made holy, so also the husband loves the wife so that she may be made holy. Now, we certainly cannot assume that this only goes one way. This is a picture that Paul paints of marriage as a reflection of Christ and the church in order to make a point. God desires for all of his children to be transformed, not just wives. Husband and wife can challenge each other to become holy and blameless as they journey through life together.

Marriage is a natural environment for change. Everyone changes in one way or another through the influence of the relationship. Think about ways you have changed through the course of your marriage. Whether a small habit, like rolling up the toothpaste tube, or a change in character, like being more aware of the feelings of others or having greater self-confidence, you are affected by your spouse.

Through the course of your relationship, what is one way your spouse has influenced you to become a better person?

If we affect each other naturally in these ways, how much more can we encourage, admonish, and pray each other into the transforming arms of Christ!

"God is so committed to our transformation. There is no better context for that to happen than in marriage." —John Eldredge

Conflict happens in marriage. It is normal. You may ask yourself, "Why is this so difficult? Why are we having this conflict?" It's because you're married. Two sinners coming together with different backgrounds, different personalities, different opinions, and their own selfish desires are naturally going to have conflict. There is no way around it. Neither you nor your spouse is perfect.

It is not easy to learn to love. It is not easy to deny your selfishness and put someone else's desires first when they are so different from your own. It is not easy to ask for forgiveness and admit wrong—and it can be even more difficult to grant forgiveness and let go of grudges when you've been deeply hurt. But what matters is what you do when conflict arises. (See *Working Together*, volume 2 of Growing a Strong Marriage, to discuss conflict in more depth.)

In his book *Meaning of Marriage*, Tim Keller says that to love is

to look at another person and get a glimpse of the person God is creating, and to say, "I see who God is making you, and it excites me! I want to be part of that. I want to partner with you and God in the journey you are taking to his throne. And when we get there, I will look at your magnificence and say, 'I always knew you could be like this. I got glimpses of it on earth, but now look at you!'" Each spouse should see the great thing that Jesus is doing in the life of their mate through the Word, the gospel. Each spouse then should give him- or herself to be a vehicle for that work and envision the day that you will stand together before God, seeing each other presented in spotless beauty and glory.

If the purpose of marriage is to become more like Christ, then your spouse is the perfect person to help shape you in this process.

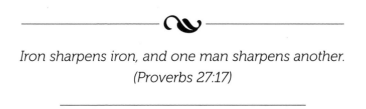

Iron sharpens iron, and one man sharpens another.
(Proverbs 27:17)

As husband and wife, you have a front-row seat to each other's life. You see the good and the bad, the annoying and the endearing, the struggles and the victories. What's typically easiest to see through—the good or the bad? It may vary depending on one's personality, but usually the bad seems to be loudest, doesn't it? But it doesn't have to be. You can choose to see who God is creating your spouse to be. Anger? God desires to transform him or her into one who is self-controlled and slow to become angry. A sharp tongue? God wants to transform him or her to be patient and of gentle speech. Worry? Laziness? God loves his children and is transforming each one. Remember who your spouse is as a child of God and who God is transforming your spouse to be. And also remember that you are on the same journey and have a long way to go as well.

Within marriage, we have the opportunity to hold each other accountable when we notice sin and areas in need of improvement in each other's life. But we must be prayerful and wise in this accountability. You cannot fix your spouse, and you are not his or her personal Holy Spirit. Sometimes it is most wise not to say anything but to let the Lord do his own work. Also important is for you to have deep enough trust with each other to be free to speak this type of truth into each other's lives. If there are other conflicts or recurring issues happening within your marriage, you are probably not in a place to tell your spouse that he/she has sin in his/her life. It may be wiser to meet with a pastor or marriage counselor to address these issues. If you do speak, remember to speak the truth in love (Ephesians 4:15) and humility, not for your own benefit, but for your spouse.

One thing you can and should do in all circumstances is to pray for your spouse. Pray that the Lord would speak to him or her and that your spouse would be transformed and renewed by the gospel. Pray that your spouse will listen as the Holy Spirit reminds him or her of his presence, peace, and provision. Pray that you also will become not only a better spouse, but that you will become more like Christ yourself and be willing to hear what rough areas need to be smoothed out in your own heart.

As Gary and Lisa Thomas explained, once we see that marriage is meant to make us holy, not happy, we gain an eternal perspective that goes beyond the happiness of the here and now. Is your spouse frustrating you and making you unhappy today? Okay, that's normal. But what does this mean for both of you for the future? Are you going to learn to listen, to love, to have empathy, to forgive? Or are you going to be so focused on your own happiness and how the other is disrupting it that the conflict remains? Conflict and tension within marriage is a great growth opportunity. It takes discipline and humility, but as you grow together through conflict and grow individually in Christ, the purpose of marriage to make you holy is being carried out.

Think back to times of growth in your life. Typically these times of significant growth tend to occur in the more difficult times rather than easy ones. Can you think of a past conflict, either small or big, in your marriage that was resolved and allowed for growth in your lives? If you both agree, share this experience with your group.

Now this idea of approaching difficulties in marriage as a means to holiness may sound nice in theory. But what about later tonight or tomorrow when this is put to the test? How easy will it be, in the midst of your frustration, to stop and say, "Oh, great! This is a growth opportunity for us to become holy." It's probably not going to happen and you probably shouldn't say this to a fuming spouse. Adopting this perspective of holiness through marriage and conflict will not occur simply by willpower. And becoming more like Christ certainly does not happen on your own. Only through God's grace and transforming power can we put aside the old self influenced by sin and put on the new self, "created after the likeness of God in true righteousness and holiness" (Ephesians 4:19–24).

Once again, let's turn to Ephesians 5:18–21. On what is this entire discussion of marriage, submitting to one another, and being made holy based?

The presence of the Holy Spirit is essential. Only through our dependence on the Holy Spirit can we truly set aside our own selfishness and submit ourselves to one another. It is then that we can see that marriage is not simply about happiness but is more about holiness. Marriage is a reflection of Christ's sacrificial love to make his church holy, and a model of how you ought to also love each other with this sacrificial love, putting your spouse's needs above your own.

As we've discussed, prayer is important as we pray for our spouse to be more like Christ and as we ourselves desire to imitate him. But the couples in the video we watched discuss another important aspect of prayer in marriage.

The Eldredges talked about the "Accuser," and the Thomases talked about the "Enemy." What do we know of this enemy? Read John 10:10 and 1 Peter 5:8.

Marriage is good, created by God, and intended to form us into greater Christlikeness and holiness. Satan is the Enemy of God. He does not like anything good and beautiful and certainly not something that is intended to make someone more holy. Be aware that Satan does not want your marriage to prosper. He does not want your spouse to speak truth into your life and for you to listen and become repentant. Instead he wants you to become defensive, cast blame, and point the finger back at your spouse and his/her faults, unwilling to admit your own shortcomings. Be careful with misinterpreting body language or a certain look. Talk to each other and be open.

As with the Eldredges, maybe there is an Accuser in your marriage who is casting lies in your mind that your spouse never even considered uttering. Maybe there is an Enemy who has trapped you two into a cycle of misunderstanding and miscommunication. How often have you jumped to conclusions, making assumptions about what was really being said, only to find yourself defensive and in the middle of needless escalation? Be diligent to listen to your spouse and the Holy Spirit, not the Accuser. Even at times when you don't yet feel reconciled, you can stand together and pray against the Enemy and for Christ to intervene and bring peace and understanding. You have become one. Fight together on the same team rather than against each other.

So what makes a Christian marriage? Is it two Christians who happen to be married? No, it is really far more than that. You are on this journey of transformation together. If you're working together, both of you will become more like Christ over time, which is better for you, each other, and your marriage. A Christian marriage is two people with their eyes fixed on Christ, devoted to joining in the fight to become more like Christ and to see each other transformed into his likeness.

Jesus did not love us because we are loveable. He loved us because that is who he is, and he chose to love us and give himself up for us. Sometimes your spouse is not loveable. But you can still choose to love him or her. Because you have received such boundless, undeserved grace from the Father, you also can now extend that grace to your spouse.

Take a short moment to share what your main take-away from this session has been.

Questions for Home

What is an area of conflict that you can mutually agree needs to change and you can work on together?

You have been reminded that your spouse is also striving for holiness as you are and that marriage is meant to make each of you more like Christ. What difference does this make in your mind? How can you remember this in your next argument?

What is an area of conflict in your marriage in which you have grown? What is another area that is still present that you would consider a waiting growth opportunity?

Notes / Prayer Requests

Notes / Prayer Requests

_____

_____

_____

_____

_____

_____

_____

_____

_____

_____

_____

_____

_____

_____

_____

_____

_____

Leader's Guide

Thank you for leading this small group for Growing a Strong Marriage! As couples gather together over the next few weeks, you have the opportunity to provide them with material that will help them to develop new ways of thinking about their marriage and themselves.

Beginning the Small Group

- The Growing a Strong Marriage series is a set of three study guides with corresponding video sessions on DVDs. Generally speaking, there is one video per session, running roughly seven to fifteen minutes each. The study guides have been developed in a way that allows the leader to customize the order of the sessions to fit the group's needs. For the most complete experience, however, it is recommended that the sessions be completed in the order in which they have been presented.

- It is recommended to keep the small groups to two to four couples in order to allow everyone adequate time to share. If you have more couples interested, encourage someone else to lead a group.

- Each session has been designed to be completed in one hour, including the video and corresponding study guide. If you have longer time to meet, you can extend the discussion or even complete two sessions back to back. If being used for a retreat, seminar, or church event, sessions can also be run one after the other.

- Lastly, please be mindful of the time. Some of the participants may have enlisted childcare in order to attend and will need to leave by a certain time. When the small group is scheduled, set a realistic time to begin and end, and do your best to hold to these times.

General Suggestions

- Some participants will be more than willing to join in discussion, while others will be more reserved. As the leader, encourage everyone to participate, respect-fully guiding the talkative and drawing out the quiet. Wisely moderate when it is appropriate to allow silence for people to think and when it is best to move on to the next section of the study guide.

- As the leader, you have the opportunity to model brevity and the appropriate answer. For the first session, be the first to share when a question is asked, demonstrating proper length of response. This can also help break the ice and make others feel comfortable.

Starting the First Session

- If the participants in the small group do not already know each other or you, begin by briefly introducing yourself and asking the participants to do the same. You can cover the basics for now: names, how long married, number of children (though be sensitive to those without children), and so on. You'll go over more details of each marriage later in the session.

- Begin with prayer, asking the Lord to speak to each person and to strengthen each marriage present.

- Read through the introduction to the series and the introduction to the study guide to help introduce Growing a Strong Marriage and what the participants can expect over the next few weeks. You can either read it beforehand and summarize, or read it together as a group.

- Start with Session 1 in the study guide and then watch the session on the DVD when prompted in the guide. After you have finished watching Session 1 on the video, return to the study guide, stopping along the way to answer the discussion questions as a group.

Continuing the Following Sessions

- For each following session, open the group in prayer. Then check in with the group and see if there are any brief comments anyone has from the previous session. Be careful to leave these comments to just a few minutes so that you will have plenty of time to cover the new material.

- Begin the next session in the study guide and watch the session on the DVD when prompted in the study guide. After the video is complete, follow along in the study guide in the same way.

Growing a
STRONG
Marriage

Whether you have been married for a few years or thirty years, there is always room to

grow.

Introducing a 3-volume study series on marriage, featuring candid interviews with your favorite relationship experts:

John & Stasi Eldredge
Chip & Theresa Ingram
Gordon & Gail MacDonald

Les & Leslie Parrott
Art & Lysa TerKeurst
Gary & Lisa Thomas